SCIENCE

THROUGH THE SEASONS

SPRING

GABRIELLE WOOLFITT

Wayland

Titles in the series

Spring
Summer
Autumn
Winter

Series editor: Katie Orchard
Series designer: Pinpoint Design
Book designer: Jean Wheeler
Artist: Pauline Allen
Production controller: Carol Stevens
Photo stylist: Zoë Hargreaves

First published in 1995 by Wayland Publishers Ltd
61 Western Road, Hove, East Sussex, BN3 1JD, England

British Library Cataloguing in Publication Data
Woolfitt, Gabrielle
Spring. – (Science Through the Seasons series)
I. Title II. Series
507.8

ISBN 0 7502 1458 9

Typeset in England by Jean Wheeler
Printed and bound by L.E.G.O. S.p.A., Vicenza, Italy

Cover pictures: A wood anemone and a starling feeding its young.
Title page picture: A blue tit feeding its young.

Contents

Words in **bold** are in the glossary on page 30.

What is Spring?

Spring is the start of nature's year. In **temperate** lands, spring starts on a day called the spring **equinox**. There are twelve hours of daylight and twelve hours of night on this day. During spring, the days get longer. Spring ends on the summer **solstice**. This is the longest day of the year.

▼ Ramsons

◀ Rabbits

Violets ▶

This North American brown bear is hungry. It has just come out of **hibernation**.

Spring follows winter. During winter, it is too cold for many plants and animals to survive. During spring, the weather gets warmer. Leaves and flowers start to grow on plants. Animals come out from their winter homes. They get into pairs and **mate**. Young animals can be seen in the woods and fields.

Signs of Spring

You can tell that winter is over when you see the first signs of spring. The sun rises early in the morning. Leaf buds start to open up on the trees. You do not need to wear so many clothes when you go out because the temperature is warmer.

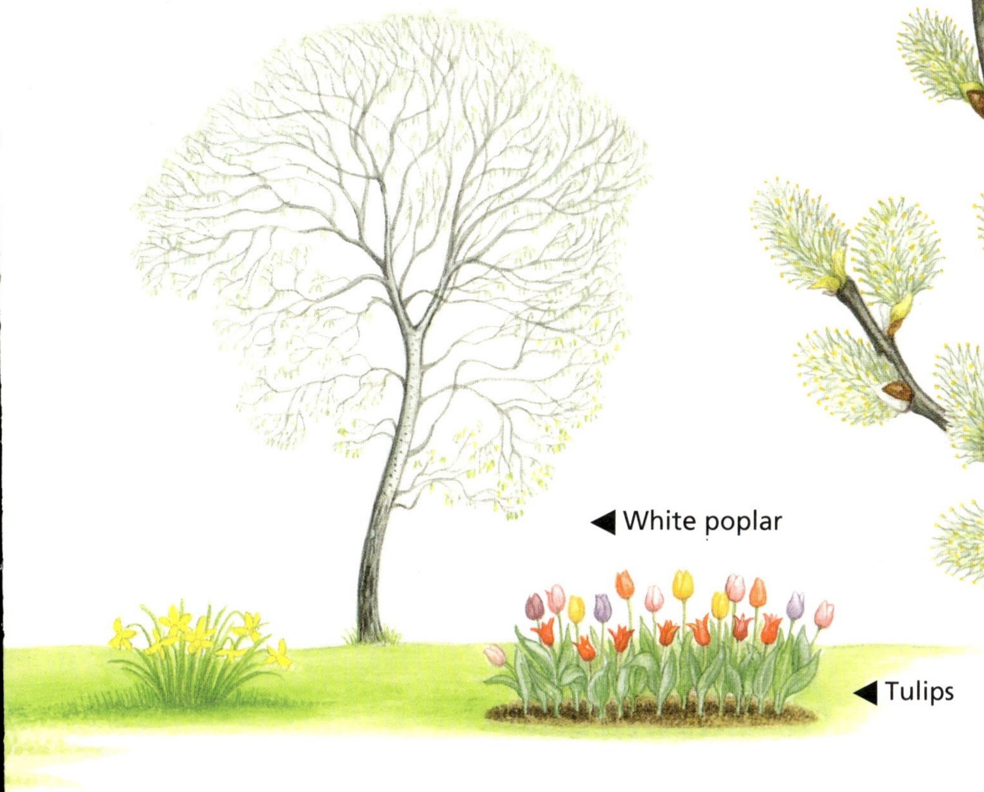

This female blackbird has found some grass to make her nest with.

Birds start to build their nests so that they can lay eggs. Spring flowers such as daffodils come into bloom. Some trees have long **catkins**. These are made up of small flowers on long stems. The **pollen** from the catkins gets blown around by the wind. Pollen from one tree can **fertilize** the catkins of other trees. The catkins make seeds. The seeds may grow into new trees if they land in soil.

Spring Around the World

In the northern **hemisphere**, spring is from March to June. In the southern hemisphere, spring is from September to December.

Countries in the **tropical** regions do not really have seasons. It is warm nearly all year round. In some places, such as Darwin in Australia, the spring temperature can be as high as 30 °C.

During the daytime in the Sahara Desert (in the north of Africa), it is hot nearly all year round.

Countries that are in the temperate regions, usually have four seasons. In spring, there is often cool weather, rain or showers. Sometimes, snow can still be seen on the ground. In Norway, snow stays on the tops of the mountains throughout spring. In the valleys, the snow melts and spring flowers come out.

In the Arctic Circle (the North **Pole**) there is no spring and only a short summer. In the Antarctic (the South Pole) it is cold all year round.

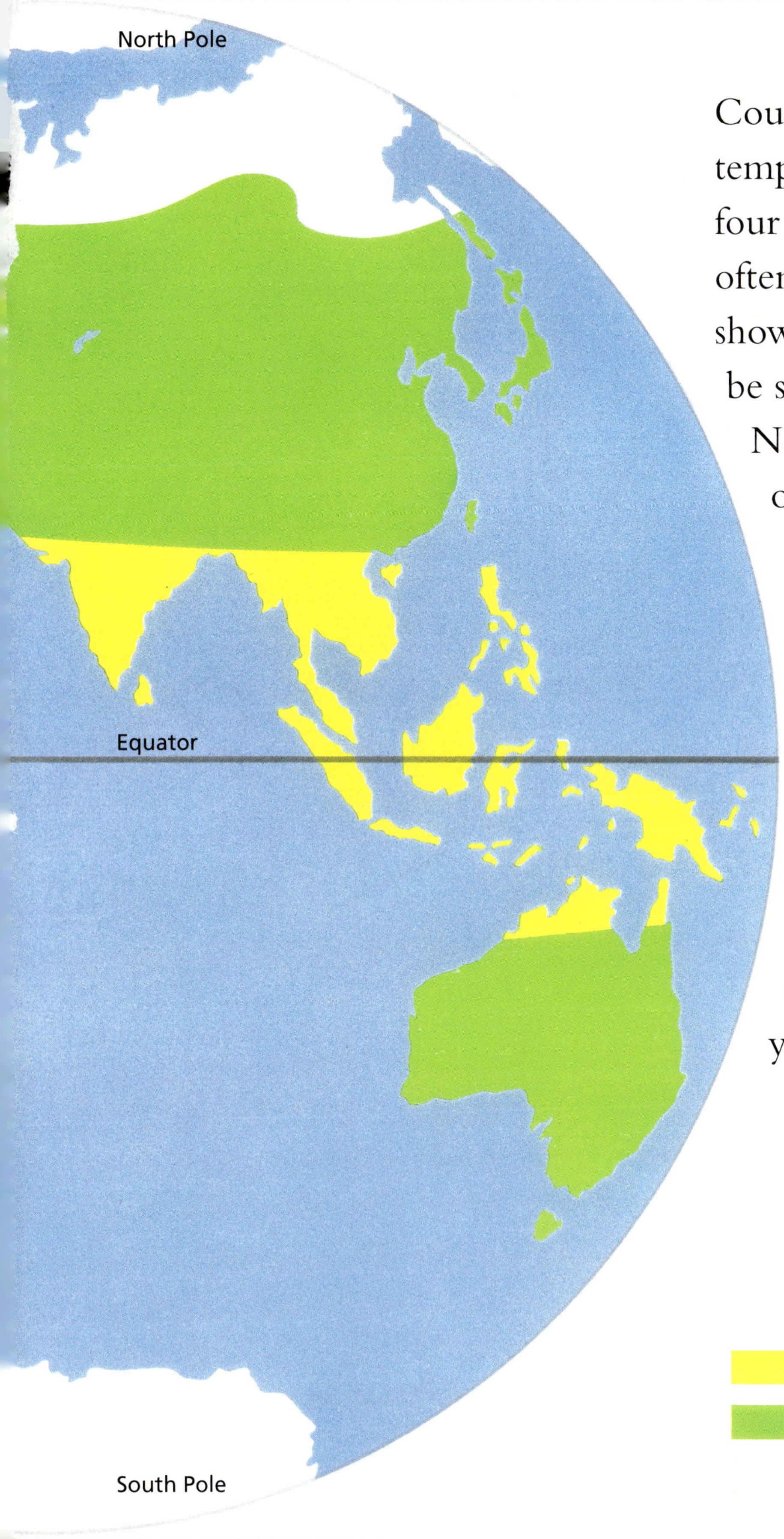

Spring Weather

In spring, the sun heats up the water in the sea. Some of the water becomes a fine mist and rises high in the sky. Droplets of water form clouds in the sky and make rain. You can measure how much rain falls near your home or school with a **rain gauge**. This activity shows you how to make a rain gauge.

1. Ask an adult to cut the top off the bottle to make a funnel shape. Turn the top upside down and fit it into the rest of the bottle. ▼

YOU WILL NEED:
a plastic bottle with a flat base, scissors, a small spade, a ruler, a pencil, paper, sticky tape.

▲ 2. Draw a **scale** on some paper in centimetres.

▲ 3. Stick the scale on the bottle with some sticky tape. Make sure the scale starts at the bottom of the bottle.

▲ 4. Dig a small hole in the garden for the bottle. Make sure that the hole is away from buildings or fences. Stand the bottle upright in the hole.

▲ 5. After one week, collect your rain gauge. Use the scale to see how much rain fell.

You could make a chart to show how much rain fell during each week of spring.

Spring Showers

In spring, there are often sudden showers. To keep dry, you will need an umbrella or a rain hat. This experiment will help you choose the best material to keep you dry.

YOU WILL NEED:
scissors, squares of different materials, such as cotton, felt, jean material, kitchen paper, cotton wool, plastic, a **pipette**, a saucer for each material, a cup of water.

▲ 1. Cut each piece of material to the same size to fit over the saucers.

▲ 2. Fill the pipette with water from the cup. Practise dropping some water back into the cup.

3. Drop the water into the middle of one of the materials. Does the water soak in or does it stay on top? ▶

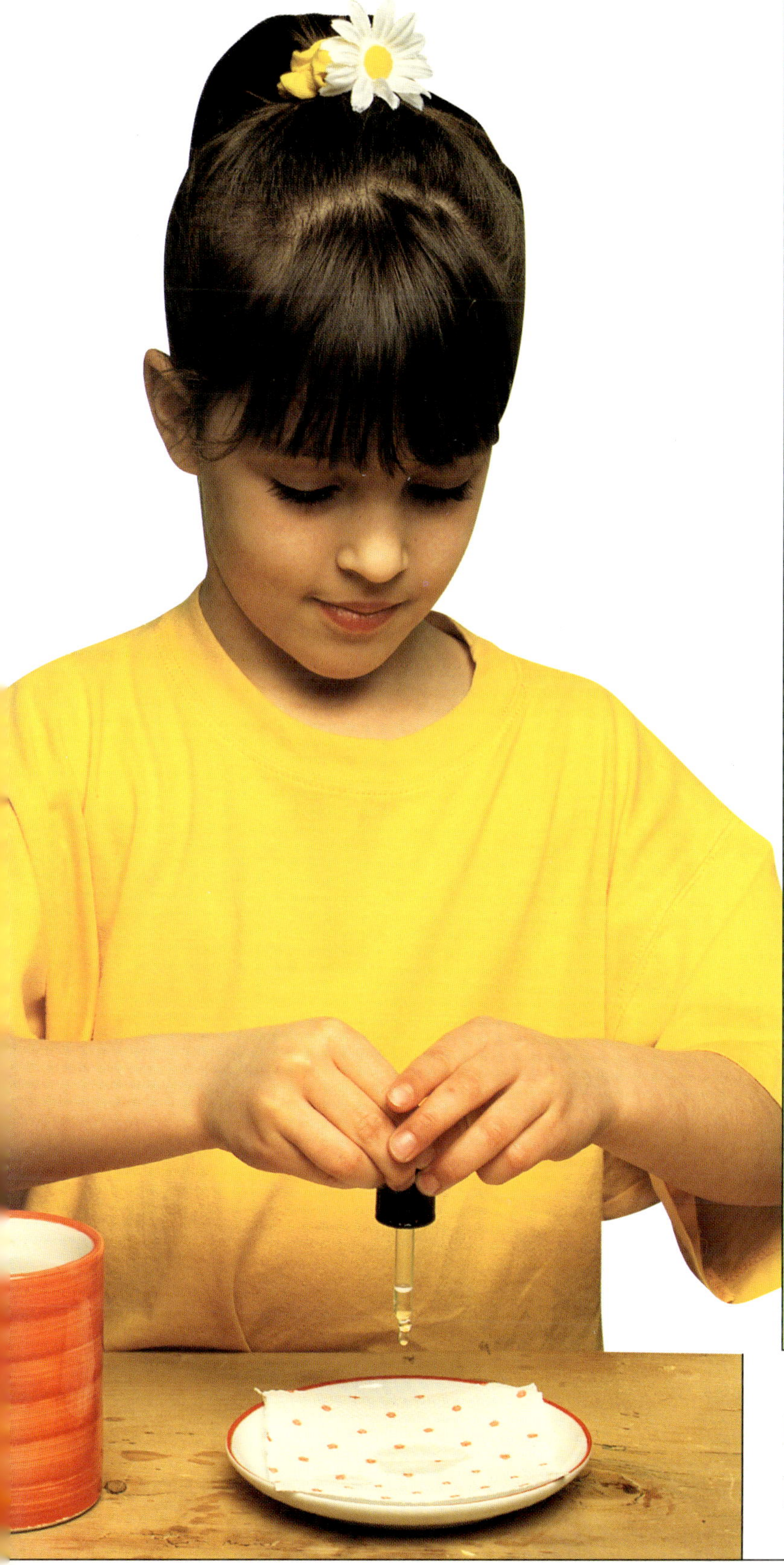

▲ 4. If the water soaks in, see how many drops it takes to completely wet the material.

▲ 5. Repeat the experiment with each material in turn. Which material would make the best umbrella? Which would be the worst?

Material needs to be waterproof to keep you dry.

Bulbs

Some plants grow from bulbs. Bulbs store food for the plant under the ground. When it gets warmer in spring the bulbs start to grow. This activity shows you how to grow your own bulbs.

YOU WILL NEED:
some iris bulbs, a wide, deep pot (at least four times as deep as the bulbs), bulb **compost**, a plant pot stand, newspaper, stones, a small spade, a watering can.

▲ 1. Put the pot and its pot stand on some newspaper. Put some stones over the holes in the pot.

▲ 2. Put a shallow layer of compost into the bottom of the pot to cover the stones.

▲ 3. Arrange each bulb with the flat end on the compost and the pointed end at the top. Leave a 4 cm gap between each bulb.

▲ 4. Bury the bulbs with more compost. Make sure that the compost goes all around each bulb.

▲ 5. Water the pot. Leave it on the pot stand on a window sill.

Your bulbs will soon grow and flower.

Blossom

Blossom is the name for the small white or pink flowers on fruit trees. Blossom is seen on fruit trees in the spring.

Pear trees are covered in white blossom in mid-spring. The leaves open a few weeks later. Wild cherry trees have pale pink blossom. The flowers open at the same time as the leaves appear. Hawthorn is a spiky tree or bush. The leaves appear in the middle of spring but the blossom comes later.

▲ Pear blossom

Beefly ▶

▼ Honey bee

◀ Apple blossom

Insects carry pollen from one blossom to another and this fertilizes the flower. The fertilized flower turns into fruit with seeds in the middle.

◀ Quince

White hawthorn ▶

Bumble bee ▼

In Tokyo, Japan, these people are enjoying the Cherry Blossom festival.

▼ Red hawthorn

▼ Plum

Wasp ▼

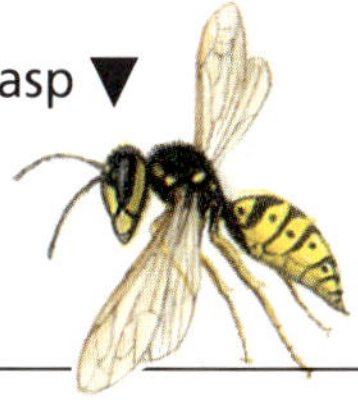

Germinating Seeds

In spring the soil warms up. Seeds need warm soil to **germinate**. Different seeds grow into different plants. This activity shows you how to grow different seeds.

▼ 1. Put both pots in their pot stands on some newspaper and fill the pots with compost.

YOU WILL NEED:

two 20 cm plant pots, six sunflower seeds, some cress seeds, potting compost, two plant pot stands, two plastic bags, two elastic bands, newspaper, a small spade, a watering can.

▲ 2. Water the compost and leave the pots to drain for half an hour.

▲ 3. Sprinkle the cress seeds on top of the compost in one pot.

▲ 4. Push the sunflower seeds into the compost of the other pot with your finger. Make sure the sunflower seeds are covered by the compost.

▲ 5. Put the plastic bags over the pots, making sure that the plants still have room to grow. Fasten the bags to the pots using the elastic bands.

▲ 6. Leave the pots somewhere warm until little **shoots** appear. When the leaves touch the plastic bags, take them off and let the plants grow in sunlight.

Seeds need to be moist to germinate. The plastic helps to keep in the moisture.

Insects and Butterflies

Insects hibernate during winter. When it gets warmer, they wake up. They are hungry. They need **nectar** to give them energy. Insects are attracted to bright flowers such as dandelions. When they have eaten enough, the insects **breed**.

This red admiral butterfly is drinking nectar. Butterflies have special long tongues to reach the nectar inside the flowers.

Butterflies lay eggs on certain kinds of plants. The eggs hatch into caterpillars which then eat the plants. By summer, the caterpillars have turned into butterflies.

Some butterflies **migrate** to warm countries. The red admiral goes to the warm countries in the south of Europe for the winter. In spring, it flies to the north of Europe to breed again.

Birds in Spring

In spring, female birds lay eggs. The egg shell protects the baby bird as it grows. These experiments will help you to find out about eggs.

YOU WILL NEED:
a hen's egg, a flat table, a bowl.

▲ 1. Put the egg in the middle of the table and roll it gently. The egg does not roll far before it goes in a curve. The more pointed the egg, the less distance it rolls.

▲ 2. Tap the egg at its flat end. It does not break easily.

Gulls lay their eggs on shelves on cliffs. They have very pointed eggs so that the eggs will not be able to roll into the sea.

▲ 4. Break the egg into a bowl by banging the middle of the egg against the edge of the bowl.

▲ 5. Look carefully at the egg. In a fertilized egg, a chick grows and feeds on the yolk. The egg white keeps the chick floating until it hatches.

▲ 3. Try tapping the pointed end. The curved shape is very strong.

It is difficult to break a full egg. This protects the baby bird inside.

Shop eggs do not grow into chicks because they have not been fertilized.

Animals in Spring

In spring, lots of animals come out of hibernation. Snails, hedgehogs, snakes and frogs can be seen in the garden. They need plenty to eat after a winter without food. Some animals mate and produce young in spring.

Frogs come out of hibernation in spring. They lay eggs called frog spawn in ponds. These eggs hatch into tiny tadpoles.

These tadpoles will soon grow and change into frogs.

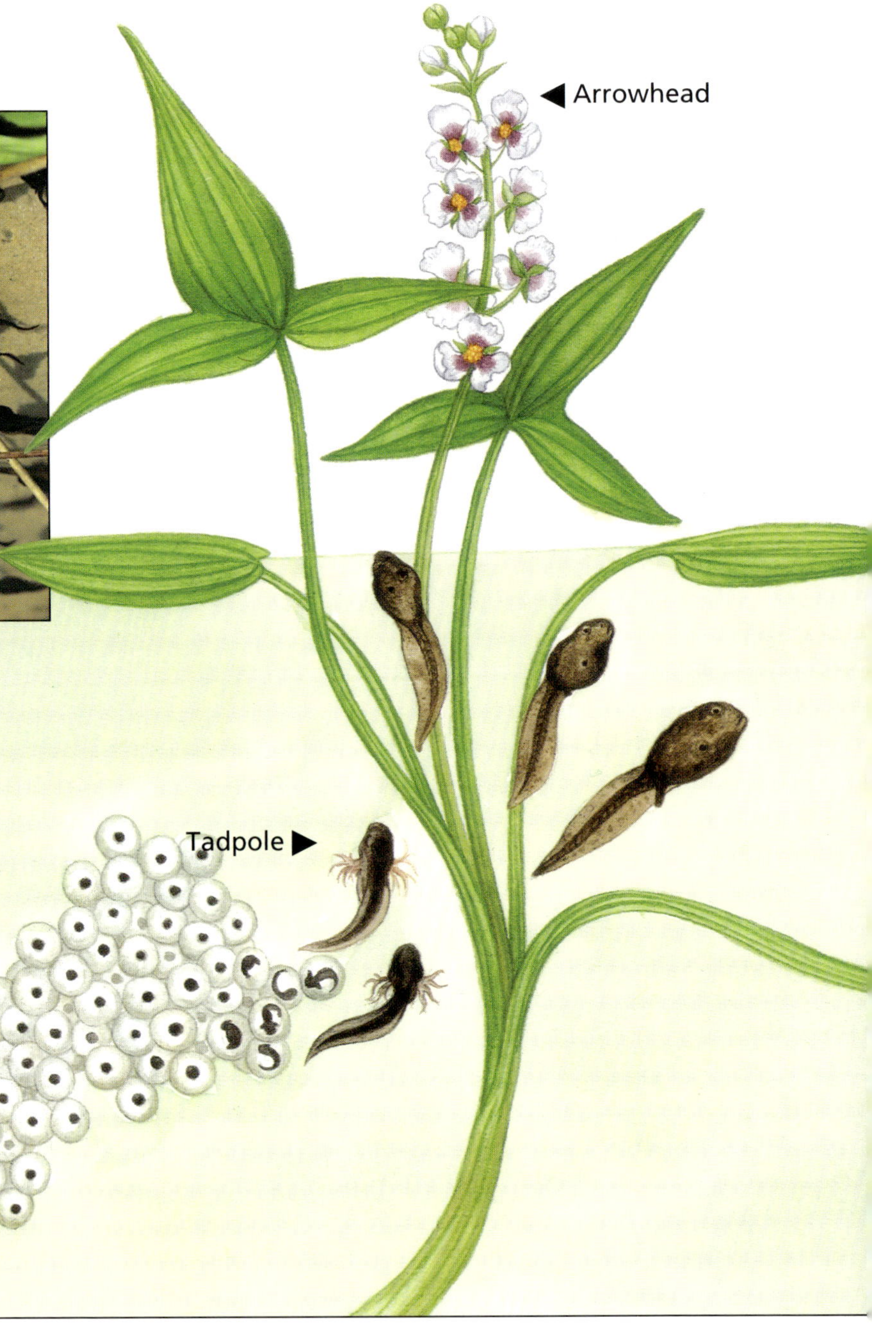

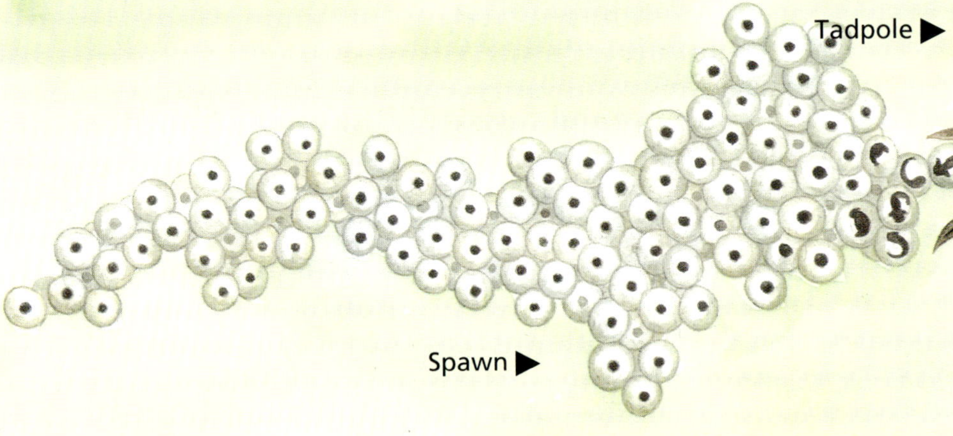

The tadpoles eat small plants in the water and gradually change into frogs. By the end of spring, the young frogs come out of the pond. They need to grow big and strong during the summer so they will be able to survive the cold winter.

(Main picture) The life cycle of the common frog, from spawn to adult.

Spring On the Farm

Spring is a very busy time on the farm. If the weather is warm, the fields will start to dry out. The farmer must wait until the puddles have dried up before the new seeds can be planted.

Leeks can stay in the ground during the winter. They are ready to eat in the spring.

When the soil is warm and not too muddy, the farmer plants seeds using a seed drill attached to a tractor. Some **crops** have grown since autumn. They are ready to **harvest**.

Animals are put out in the fields to eat grass. The lambs which were born at the end of winter are getting bigger. They can now join the rest of the flock.

Get Ready for Summer

By the end of spring, all the trees have leaves. The days are long and warm. You can hear insects buzzing around the flowers. The seeds that you planted in pots at the start of spring will be ready to plant in the garden. You can see the small apples growing on apple trees. Baby birds start to leave the nest. Watch them learn to fly.

These tiny starlings are fed by their parents until they are able to fly.

In the countryside, the crops are growing taller. Young deer become less timid and leave their mothers' sides.

In three months everything has changed. The cold snow of winter has gone. All the birds and insects have had young. The summer flowers are ready to open. Summer has arrived.

Glossary

breed To produce young.

catkins Tiny flowers that hang down in clusters on certain types of trees.

compost Soil which is very rich in plant food.

crops Plants grown on a farm for food.

equinox When the day and the night are the same length. This happens twice a year.

fertilize When a male plant or animal passes on a special seed to a female of the same species that makes her produce a young plant or animal.

germinate To begin to grow.

harvest To gather crops when they are ripe.

hemisphere Half the globe. The two hemispheres are called the northern and southern hemispheres.

hibernation Sleeping for a long time during the cold weather. Animals and insects that hibernate wake up in spring.

mate When a male and a female get into a pair to produce young.

migrate To move to a warmer country in winter.

nectar A sweet liquid found inside flowers. Bees collect nectar to make honey.

pipette An instrument used to make very small droplets of liquid.

Pole The name for the places in the world that are furthest north and furthest south. These are called the North Pole and the South Pole.

pollen The yellow powder inside a flower. Pollen helps to make seeds.

rain gauge An instrument used to measure the amount of rainfall.

scale A form of measurement.

shoots The first signs of growth in a plant.

solstice The longest day of the year is the summer solstice. The shortest day is the winter solstice.

temperate A word used to describe countries that have four seasons.

tropical Regions that are hot all year round.

Books to Read

Be Your Own Weather Expert by J. Kelly (Simon and Schuster, 1991)

Science Activities: Meteorology by Graham Peacock (Wayland, 1994)

Spring Weather by John Mason (Wayland, 1990)

Wasteland by Colin S. Milkins (Wayland, 1994)

The Weather by T. Potter (BBC Books, 1989)

The World's Weather by David Flint (Wayland, 1992)

Picture acknowledgements

Ecoscene 20; Eye Ubiquitous *cover* (far right), 17 © Jim Holmes, 27 © Ken Oldroyd, 28 © Mostyn 92; Frank Lane Picture Agency 5 © Mark Newman, 7 © R. Wilmshurst, 24 © Eric & David Hosking; Oxford Scientific Films 8 © Richard Packwood; Wayland Picture Library *cover* (photograph by Colin S. Milkins) far left, *back cover* (photograph by Colin S. Milkins) top left, *title page* (photograph by Colin S. Milkins).

The commissioned photographs used in this book were taken by APM Studios.

The publishers would like to thank the staff and children at Somerhill School, Hove, Sussex for their kind assistance.

Index